Mighty
SHIPS

IAN GRAHAM

W

FRANKLIN WATTS
LONDON • SYDNEY

 An Appleseed Editions book

First published in 2006 by Franklin Watts

Reprinted 2006

Franklin Watts
338 Euston Road, London NW1 3BH

Franklin Watts Australia
Level 17/207 Kent St, Sydney, NSW 2000

© 2006 Appleseed Editions

Appleseed Editions Ltd
Well House, Friars Hill, Guestling, East Sussex TN35 4ET

Created by Q2A Creative
Editor: Chester Fisher
Designer: Mini Dhawan
Picture Researchers: Simmi Sikka, Somnath Bhowmick

ISBN 0 7496 6752 4

Dewey Classification: 623.8'2

A CIP catalogue for this book is available from the British Library.

Picture credits
t=top b=bottom c=centre l=left r=right
Half title: Official U.S. Navy Photo, Aker Finnyards: 22b, 23b, Andreas Vallbracht: 12-13b,
Bob Lendrum: 4t, Cunard Line: 12t, 12c, Dockwise Shipping B.V.: 24b,
Frank Poppe: 23t, Freedom Ship International, Inc: 29t, Gettyimages: 26b,
Haze Gray & Underway: 25t, 25c, Ian Sewell: 8t, Incat: 20b, Kev Belcher: 9t,
Naval Historical Center: 17c, Official US Navy Photo: 5b, 16b, 17t, 17b, 20t, 27t, 27b,
Paul Labine, Canadian Merchant Marine: 19t, Risto: 21b, Rolls-Royce plc: 7t, 13t, 28b,
SCHOTTEL GmbH & Co. KG: 7br, Science Museum / Science & Society Picture Library: 10b, 11t, 11b,
The Cutty Sark Trust: 9b, Volga shipyard-Russia: 14b, www.boeingiplicensing.com: 15t,
www.freefoto.com: 21t, www.royalcaribbeanimagelibrary.com: 6-7b.

Printed in Singapore

Franklin Watts is a division of Hachette Children's Books.

CONTENTS

MIGHTY SHIPS

Ships are vital for world trade. They transport most of the goods and materials that are traded around the world.

TYPES OF SHIPS

There are about 45,000 cargo ships and passenger ships on the seas. Some of them are ferries carrying people on short sea journeys. Others are liners taking passengers on floating holidays. Most of the big vessels, however, are cargo ships carrying a wide variety of products. Another 37,000 ships are used for fishing.

Fishing trawler

Warship

Cruise liner

Cargo ship

Cargo ships dock every day at busy ports with goods and materials from all over the world.

FAST FACTS
Working Ships
Ships that carry goods, materials or paying passengers between countries are also called merchant ships.

Modern destroyers are fast and deadly warships.

WARSHIPS

The warships of the world's navies patrol the oceans. During wartime, the warships battle for control of the sea and carry equipment and troops to where they are needed. Some of the biggest ships afloat today are warships with crews of up to 6,000 people.

HOW SHIPS WORK

Modern ships are complicated floating machines. Their size, shape, speed and power depend on the jobs they are designed to do.

Engine exhausts
Let smoke and fumes from the engines escape

Radar dome
Tracking ship's position

SHIP SHAPE

The part of a ship that sits in the water is called its hull. Its shape is carefully designed so that it glides easily through water. A slim hull slices through water faster than a fat hull, but a slim hull has less space inside. Cargo ships usually have fat hulls to hold more cargo.

Engines
Drive the ship's propellers and electricity generators

Most ships steer by turning a rudder. Water pushes against it and swings the ship round. Some ships steer by swivelling their propellers. Ships with waterjet engines steer by turning the jets.

Hull
Made from steel

Decks
For passenger cabins, restaurants and theatres

Propellers
Power the ship through the water

This Rolls-Royce UT-740 fire-and-rescue ship also delivers supplies to oil and gas drilling rigs.

Engine
Most ships are powered by diesel engines

RESCUE ZONE

UT 740

ENGINES

Most ships are powered by diesel engines, like the engines in giant trucks. The engines turn the propellers and the blades of the propeller push against the water and drive the ship forwards. Some ships have gas turbine engines. They work like an airliner's jet engines, but they turn propellers. Other ships have waterjet engines.

Some ships have extra propellers called thrusters to help them manoeuvre. A cowling protects the blades.

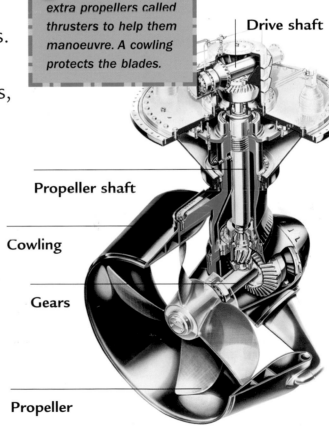

Drive shaft

Propeller shaft

Cowling

Gears

Propeller

Bridge
The ship's control centre

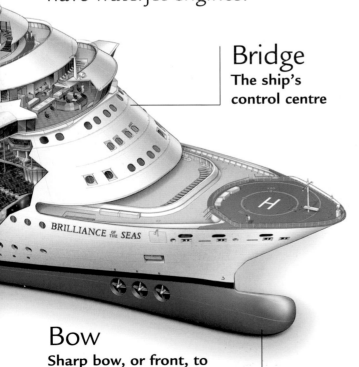

BRILLIANCE OF THE SEAS

Bow
Sharp bow, or front, to slice through the water

FAST FACTS
Sea Speed
A ship's speed is measured in knots. A knot is one nautical mile per hour, or 1.852 kph (1.15 mph).

THE FIRST SHIPS

No one knows when the first ship was built, but we know that people have been building ships for thousands of years.

ANCIENT SHIPS

Today, there is nothing left of the earliest ships. They were made of wood and they rotted away long ago. But parts of ships more than 6,400 years old have been found. The oldest whole ship we have today was built about 4,600 years ago for the funeral of an Egyptian pharaoh called Khufu.

Khufu's funeral ship was built for the dead pharaoh to use in the after-life.

Masts
Carry the sails

Sails
Catch the wind

Hull
Made from wooden planks

The great voyages of discovery were made in wooden sailing ships. The wind filled their sails and blew them across the oceans to new lands.

HMS Victory was built from the wood of more than 2,000 oak trees.

Sails
A total of 32 made from canvas

Rigging
43 kilometres of rope

Gun ports
Opened for cannons to fire through

Quarter deck
Where the officers stood and shouted their orders

Officers' cabins
Where the officers slept

Cannons
A total of 104 on three gun decks

THE AGE OF SAIL

Sailing ships explored the oceans and their crews discovered new lands. The biggest and most powerful sailing vessels were warships like HMS *Victory*. This was Admiral Nelson's famous flagship at the Battle of Trafalgar in 1805. Ships like the *Victory*, armed with cannons, fought each other in sea battles.

FAST FACTS

Clipper Ships
The tea clipper Cutty Sark *was a fast cargo ship launched in 1869. It brought tea from China to England in the 1870s and then wool from Australia.*

STEAM POWER

Early sailing ships could only get going when the wind blew and they could only go where the wind blew them. The steam engine gave ships their own power.

FIRST STEAMSHIPS

Early steamships had paddlewheels. The engine turned a big wheel on each side of the ship. However, paddlewheels were easily damaged and they did not work well in rough water. When a boat rolled to one side, the paddlewheel on the other side lifted out of the water.

Paddles
Pushed the water to move a ship

Early steamships were propelled by big wheels called paddlewheels.

The Great Eastern was the biggest ship that had ever been built when it was launched in 1858. It was 211 metres long.

Two British warships called Alecto and Rattler had a tug of war in 1845. The propeller-powered Rattler won and proved that propellers are better than paddlewheels.

Engine
519 horsepower steam engine

Propeller
3 metres across

TURBINE POWER

As Queen Victoria watched some warships in 1897, a boat called *Turbinia* steamed up and down the lines of ships. It wasn't supposed to be there, but it was so fast that no one could catch it. It had a new engine called a steam turbine. A turbine is a drum with blades sticking out. When steam hits the blades, the turbine spins and turns the propeller.

Turbinia's turbine engine made it faster than any warship of that time.

FAST FACTS
Sail and Steam
Early steamships had sails as well as a steam engine in case the engine broke down.

LINERS

The most comfortable way to travel long distances is by spacious passenger ships called liners.

Queen Mary 2

The world's biggest liner is the *Queen Mary 2*. It's the tallest, longest, widest, heaviest and most expensive passenger ship ever built. It carries up to 2,620 passengers on 17 decks. There's enough space inside for shops, a theatre, a library and ten restaurants. It also has five swimming pools!

Hull
345 metres long

Lifeboats
Turn themselves upright if they capsize

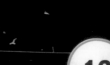

Queen Mary 2's *mermaids* propel the 150,000–tonne ship at up to 30 knots, or 55 kph (35 mph).

Mermaid
Contains an electric motor driving a propeller

MERMAID POWER

Queen Mary 2 is powered through the water by mermaids! A mermaid is a pod containing an electric motor. The motor drives a propeller. The mermaids can turn to steer the ship. *Queen Mary 2* has four mermaids. There are also three propellers called thrusters built into its bow for steering the giant ship in port.

FAST FACTS
Making Electricity
Queen Mary 2's engines are as powerful as nearly 200 racing cars. They drive generators to make electricity. At full power these make enough electricity to light a small city.

Radar
Detects nearby ships and coasts

The Queen Mary 2 carries passengers in great luxury across the Atlantic Ocean. The ship and its passengers are looked after by a crew of 1,253.

Queen Mary 2

CUNARD

FLYING SHIPS

Ships are very heavy, but some ships are actually designed to fly above the water! They are called hydrofoils.

UNDERWATER WINGS

When a hydrofoil speeds up, it rises until its hull is out of the water. Hydrofoils can fly because they have underwater wings called foils. As the foils cut through the water, they lift the ship's hull. When a hydrofoil's hull is above the water, it can go faster than other ships.

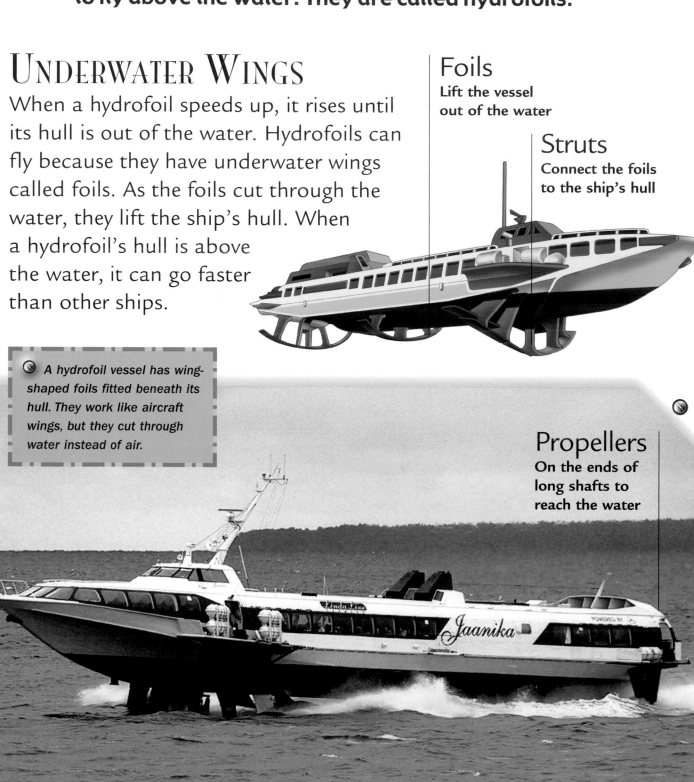

Foils
Lift the vessel out of the water

Struts
Connect the foils to the ship's hull

A hydrofoil vessel has wing-shaped foils fitted beneath its hull. They work like aircraft wings, but they cut through water instead of air.

Propellers
On the ends of long shafts to reach the water

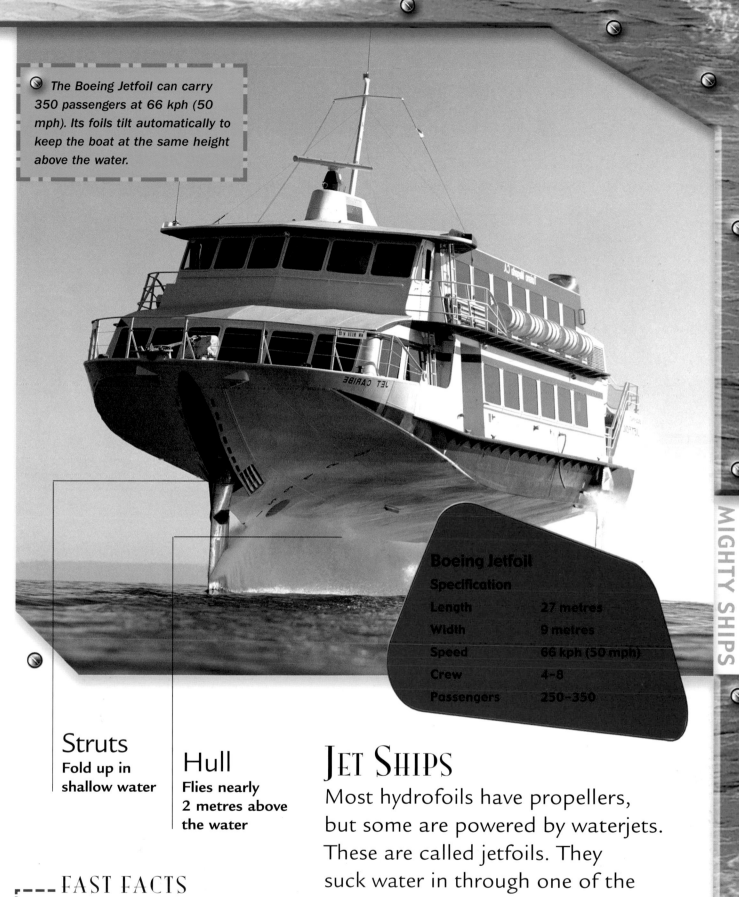

The Boeing Jetfoil can carry 350 passengers at 66 kph (50 mph). Its foils tilt automatically to keep the boat at the same height above the water.

Boeing Jetfoil
Specification

Length	27 metres
Width	9 metres
Speed	66 kph (50 mph)
Crew	4–8
Passengers	250–350

Struts
Fold up in shallow water

Hull
Flies nearly 2 metres above the water

JET SHIPS

Most hydrofoils have propellers, but some are powered by waterjets. These are called jetfoils. They suck water in through one of the underwater foils and shoot it out of the back of the ship to power it forwards. They steer like planes, by leaning over into a turn.

FAST FACTS
First Hydrofoil
The first successful hydrofoil was built in Italy by Enrico Forlanini in about 1900. It reached 68 kph (42 mph), an amazing speed for a boat at that time.

WARSHIPS

Some of the biggest, fastest and most powerful ships are warships. They have to be able to work reliably in all types of weather and in dangerous conditions.

FLOATING AIRPORTS

The biggest warships are the US Navy's Nimitz class aircraft carriers. They are giant nuclear-powered ships with crews of 6,000. These ships are floating airports that can carry warplanes anywhere in the world. Each ship is 332 metres long and weighs 92,000 tonnes .

Aircraft
Up to 85 planes and helicopters

Aerials
Pick up radio signals from ships, planes and satellites

Deck
Has a runway for planes marked on it

Island
The ship's control centre

A Nimitz class aircraft carrier stands as high as an 18-storey building.

BATTLESHIPS

Battleships used to be the biggest and most fearsome fighting ships in any navy. They had huge guns that could turn in any direction. They roamed the oceans destroying anything that got in their way. Battleships are not being built today because warships don't need big guns any more. Smaller warships armed with missiles are just as deadly.

The USA was the last country to have battleships. The USS Iowa was one of its last battleships. It served until 1991.

USS *Iowa*
Fires all its big guns at the same time

Cruise missile
Launched from a modern cruiser

FAST FACTS
Take-off
Planes launched by an aircraft carrier's catapult reach 265 kph (165 mph) in two seconds!

CARGO VESSELS

Ships carry cargo all over the world. Some cargo ships carry all sorts of different goods. Others are built specially to transport one type of cargo.

SEA GIANTS

The biggest cargo ships are oil tankers called Ultra Large Crude Carriers (ULCCs). Their vast decks are three or four times the length of a football pitch. The crews sometimes use bicycles to get around! These ships can't fit into most ports, so they have to be loaded and unloaded at special oil terminals.

Bridge
Looks out over the deck

Tanks
Filled with oil

Even a small tanker like this can carry over 10,000 tonnes of oil.

Gas carrier ships transport gases including liquefied natural gas (LNG) in huge ball-shaped tanks. The gas is changed to a liquid for the voyage, because liquid takes up less space.

FAST FACTS
Tanker Giant
The biggest ship in the world is an oil tanker called Jahre Viking. *It is 458 metres long and weighs more than half a million tonnes fully loaded.*

CONTAINER SHIPS

Most of the goods that are transported by sea are packed into standard cargo containers. The containers are the same size and shape. The ships that carry them are called container ships. The biggest container ships can carry more than 5,000 containers, each 6 metres long. Even bigger container ships are now being built.

Cargo containers are piled high on a container ship's deck. They also fill its holds. When it docks at a container port, cranes lift the containers out and pile them on the dockside.

FERRIES

Ferries are ships that carry passengers across short stretches of water. Some ferries have enough room inside to carry the passengers' cars, too.

TWIN HULLS

Cat Link V is one of the world's fastest ferries. It carries up to 900 passengers at 80 kph (50 mph). It has two thin hulls, because thin hulls cut through water fast. *Cat Link V* has no propellers or rudder. Instead, waterjets power it through the water and swivel to steer it.

Twin hulls
Cut through the waves

Passenger decks
With seating on two decks

Waterjet engines
Provide power and steering

Bridge
The ship's control centre

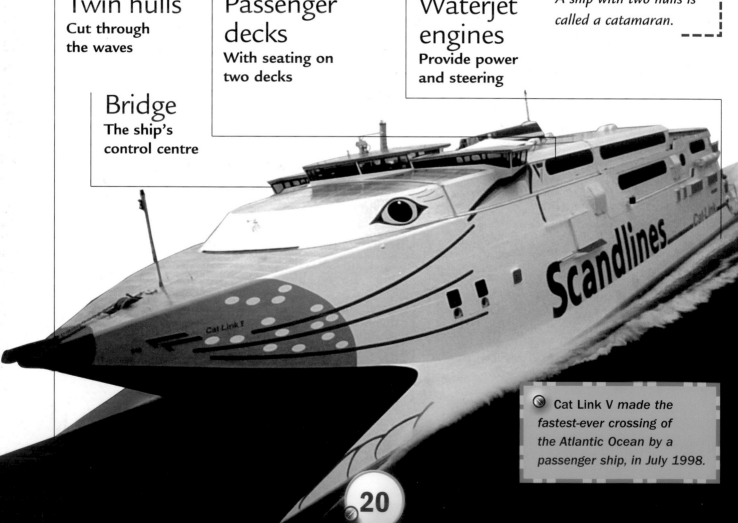

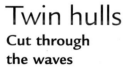

Cat Link V *made the fastest-ever crossing of the Atlantic Ocean by a passenger ship, in July 1998.*

ROLL ON, ROLL OFF

Cars used to be loaded one by one onto ships by cranes, and this took a long time. Modern ferries are designed for faster loading. They are called roll on, roll off ferries, or ro-ros. Doors in the bow (front), or stern (back), open to let vehicles drive straight in. The doors have to be strong and watertight to stop the sea from flooding in.

A SuperSeaCat leaves the port of Liverpool. It is a fast ferry made from lightweight aluminium instead of steel, because a lightweight ship goes faster than a heavy ship.

Vehicle decks
Two decks hold up to 175 cars

Hull
A deep v-shape 100 metres long

Roll on, roll off ferries have one or more decks just for cars. The passenger decks are separate from the vehicle decks.

Stern door
Opens for loading when the ship docks

ICE BREAKERS

Ice breakers are the only ships in the world that can sail through rock-hard ice without being damaged or sunk.

WHEN IS A SHIP AN ICE BREAKER?

Ships stay away from ice because ice can punch a hole in the hull. Ships can also be surrounded and crushed by ice. Ice breakers get through ice because they have three things that other ships don't have – a very strong hull, extra-powerful engines and the right shape to break ice.

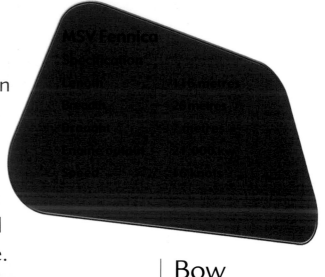

MSV Fennica
Specification

Bow
Angled to ride up onto the ice

Hull
Smooth underneath to slide easily over ice

> Ice breakers have a specially strengthened hull to withstand being battered by ice.

> Ice breakers can sail through ice that stops other ships. Ports in the far north depend on them to keep the sea-lanes open when the water freezes every winter.

Bubbles

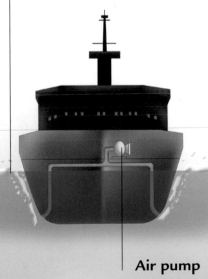

Air pump

CRACKING WORK

An ice breaker works by charging into the ice so that the bow rises up on top of it. The angled bow is exactly the right shape for this. The weight of the ship cracks the ice. Some ice breakers bubble air between the hull and ice to let the ship push through the ice more easily.

> Most ice breakers are small ships that work near the coast, but some are much bigger ocean-going ice-breaking ships.

FAST FACTS
Packed with Power
For their size, ice breakers are the most powerful ships on Earth.

SHIP CARRIERS

Some ships are designed to sink! They are strange-looking ships specially built for transporting other ships.

RESCUE SHIP

When a ship breaks down, it is usually towed to a port for repair. If it can't be towed, a special ship called a semi-submersible may come to the rescue. A semi-submersible operates partly underwater. The *Blue Marlin* is a semi-submersible that can lift and carry huge loads.

The Blue Marlin *was re-built in 2004, making it the world's biggest semi-submersible ship.*

Deck
Sinks 16 metres under the waves for loading

Hull
224 metres long

Two mine hunter ships are loaded on Blue Marlin's deck.

Cargo
Each ship weighs 895 tonnes

Cradles
Support the weight of the ships

Bow section
Contains 38 cabins for crew and passengers

BLUE MARLIN

Blue Marlin brought a warship called the USS *Cole* back to the USA after it was damaged in the Middle East. It sailed alongside the *Cole* and sank until the sea flooded over its deck. Then it moved under the *Cole* and rose up again. The *Cole* was left high and dry on the *Blue Marlin's* deck for the voyage home.

FAST FACTS
Weightlifting

Blue Marlin *and her sister ship,* Black Marlin, *were designed to transport enormous offshore drilling rigs. They can also carry ships and other structures weighing up to 73,000 tonnes.*

SPECIAL VESSELS

Some ships look different, or strange, because they were built to test something new or to make a record-breaking voyage.

OCEAN ADVENTURER

The *Adventurer* was built to set a new record for travelling round the world. Its super-slim hull is very fast, but it also rolls a lot at sea. To keep it steady, it has a small float on each side. It was the first powered vessel to go round the world in less than 80 days, breaking the old record by nine days.

Engines
Two 350 horsepower diesels

Fuel tanks
Hold up to 12 tonnes of fuel

Float
Holds the hull steady

Adventurer is made from a special plastic material that is light and also very strong.

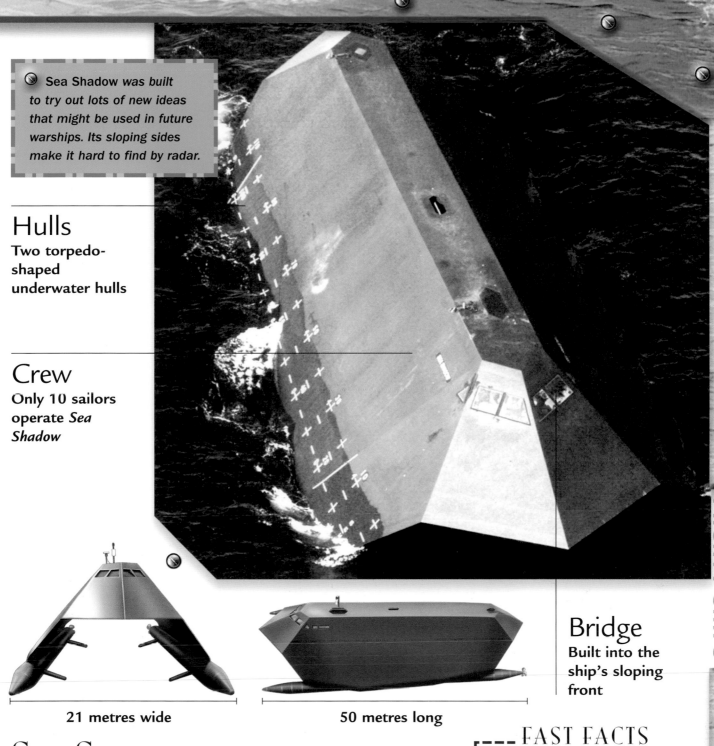

Sea Shadow *was built to try out lots of new ideas that might be used in future warships. Its sloping sides make it hard to find by radar.*

Hulls
Two torpedo-shaped underwater hulls

Crew
Only 10 sailors operate *Sea Shadow*

21 metres wide

50 metres long

Bridge
Built into the ship's sloping front

SEA SHADOW
Big metal things like ships are easy to find by using radar. Radio waves are fired out in all directions. They bounce off ships, which show up as bright spots on a radar screen. Navies would like to have warships that can hide from radar. *Sea Shadow*'s strange shape helps it to disappear from radar screens.

FAST FACTS
World Record
Before Adventurer, *the round-the-world speed record was held by the US nuclear submarine* Triton.

27

FUTURE SHIPS

Engineers are already designing the ships of the future. Some will be giant ocean-going passenger vessels. Others will be super-fast cargo transporters.

FastShip

Changing the shape of a ship's hull can make it go faster. A new ship called FastShip has a very fast hull. As it speeds up, it rises and skims across the top of the water. It will cross the Atlantic Ocean twice as fast as today's cargo ships. Its waterjet engines are as powerful as two Jumbo Jets, but a FastShip can carry 60 times more cargo than the two planes.

Engines
Five waterjets

Hull
262 metres long

Cargo
Up to 9,070 tonnes

Stern
Wide and flat for high speed

A FastShip can keep going at full speed through waves up to 15 metres high.

FastShip

Airport on
top deck

Residents' apartments

Yacht marina
in stern

Freedom Ship *will
be the biggest ship ever
built. It will be so big that
people will move around
inside it by light railway!*

FAST FACTS
Engine Power
Freedom Ship *will be powered
by 100 engines.*

LIFE ON THE OCEAN'S WAVES
Today, people go on cruises that last
a few days or weeks, but in the future some
people might live for years in giant sea-
going vessels. A ship called *The World* with
165 homes has already been built. Another
future ship called *Freedom Ship* will have
homes, shops, a school, a hospital and
businesses for up to 100,000 people. It will
circle the world every three years.

TIMELINE

4434 BC

A ship sinks off the south coast of England. Parts of its wooden hull will be found 6,431 years later, in 1997.

2600 BC

A great wooden ship is buried in Egypt for the dead Pharaoh Khufu to use in the after-life.

AD 1100

The magnetic compass is used to find the right way to steer a ship.

1802

The *Charlotte Dundas* is the world's first successful steam-powered vessel.

1819

The *Savannah* is the first steamship to cross the Atlantic Ocean.

1843

The *Great Britain* is the first large ship to have an iron hull and the first propeller-driven ship to cross the Atlantic Ocean.

1845

Two ships, *Alecto* and *Rattler*, have a tug of war to find out if paddlewheels or propellers are stronger.

1857

The giant iron ship *Great Eastern* is five times as big as any other ship.

1860

The British warship HMS *Warrior* is the first big warship to have an iron hull.

1863

The paddle steamer *Persia* is the first liner to have an iron hull.

1897

Turbinia is the first ship with a steam turbine engine.

1899

HMS *Viper* is the world's first warship to be powered by steam turbines.

1901

The first hydrofoil is built by Enrico Forlanini in Italy.

1906

The British warship HMS *Dreadnought* is the first battleship with steam turbine engines, making her the world's fastest battleship.

1932

The French liner *Normandie* is the first ship more than 313 metres (1,000 feet) long.

1958

The *Hawaiian Merchant* is the world's first container ship.

1959

The ice breaker *Lenin* is the first nuclear-powered ship.

1962

The first Boeing Jetfoil hydrofoil is launched.

1972

The first Nimitz class aircraft carrier, USS *Nimitz*, is launched.

1981

The world's biggest oil tanker, the *Seawise Giant* (now called *Jahre Viking*), is built.

2003

The *Queen Mary 2* passenger liner is launched.

GLOSSARY

bow
The front part of a ship, usually pointed.

bridge
The part of a ship where the captain and officers control the ship's movements. The bridge is raised above the rest of the ship to give a good view all round.

container ship
A cargo ship that carries cargo packed in standard containers.

diesel engine
A type of engine often used by ships. It is named after its inventor, Rudolf Diesel, and it burns a fuel called diesel oil.

horsepower
A unit for measuring the power of an engine.

hull
The part of a ship that sits in the water.

hydrofoil
A type of ship with underwater wings that lift its hull up out of the water to travel faster.

ice breaker
A type of ship specially designed for smashing its way through ice.

jetfoil
Hydrofoil powered by waterjet engines.

liner
A type of passenger ship for carrying passengers on long sea voyages and floating holidays.

merchant ship
A trading ship, or a ship that carries paying passengers or cargo.

nuclear power
A way of propelling a ship by using heat given out by natural materials, such as uranium.

radar
A way of finding a ship, even if you can't see it, by bouncing radio waves off it. Ships appear on a radar screen as bright spots.

ro-ro
A roll on, roll off ferry. A type of ship that vehicles can drive straight onto through big doors.

stealth ship
A type of warship designed to disappear from enemy radar screens.

stern
The back end of a ship.

tanker
A type of ship for transporting liquids such as oil or chemicals.

turbine
A device with lots of blades sticking out from a drum or hub. When steam hits the blades, the turbine spins fast. Ships use turbines to turn propellers or drive electricity generators.

ULCC
An Ultra Large Crude Carrier. The biggest of all the oil tankers.

waterjet engine
A ship's engine that works by sucking water in and then shooting it out very fast to move a ship.

watertight
Able to keep water out. Watertight doors stop water passing through.

INDEX

WEBFINDER

http://www.transport-pf.or.jp/english/sea/index.html *Information about ships, ports, and safety at sea*

http://www.nmm.ac.uk/TudorExploration/NMMFLASH/index.htm *Find out about Tudor ships and their great sea voyages*

http://www.cunard.co.uk/QM2 *Have a look round the world's biggest ocean liner,* Queen Mary 2

http://www.royal-navy.mod.uk/static/pages/3512.html *Find out about HMS* Victory, *the oldest commissioned warship*

http://www.rnli.org.uk/young.asp *Information, games and other stuff about lifeboats*

http://www.freedomship.com *Information on the amazing future floating city,* Freedom Ship, *with photos*

http://science.howstuffworks.com/aircraft-carrier.htm *Find out how the world's biggest warships work*

http://www.onr.navy.mil/focus/ocean/resources/sinkingships.htm *A simple experiment to know why ships float*